States

SOUTH DAKOTA

by Bridget Parker

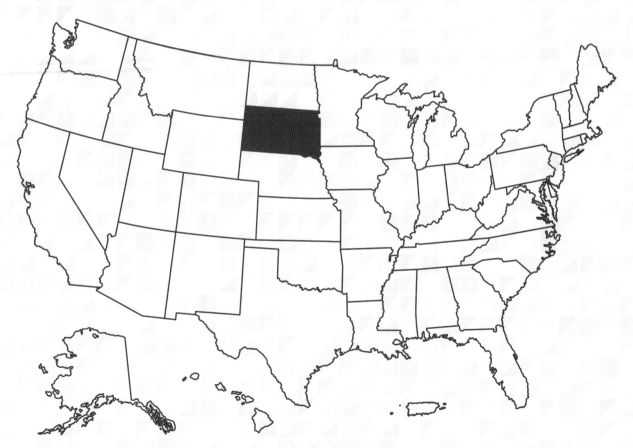

CAPSTONE PRESS
a capstone imprint

Next Page Books are published by Capstone Press,
1710 Roe Crest Drive, North Mankato, Minnesota 56003
www.mycapstone.com

Library of Congress Cataloging-in-Publication Data
Cataloging-in-publication information is on file with the Library of
Congress.
ISBN 978-1-5157-0429-4 (library binding)
ISBN 978-1-5157-0488-1 (paperback)
ISBN 978-1-5157-0540-6 (ebook PDF)

Editorial Credits
Jaclyn Jaycox, editor; Kazuko Collins and Katy LaVigne, designers;
Morgan Walters, media researcher; Tori Abraham, production specialist

Photo Credits
Capstone Press: Angi Gahler, map 4, 7; Corbis: Bettmann, bottom 18,
Marilyn Angel Wynn/Nativestock Pictures, 16; CriaImages.com: Jay
Robert Nash Collection, middle 19; Dreamstime: Bradley Dailey, 10,
28, Martin Ellis, top 18; Glow Images: SuperStock, top 19; Newscom:
Everett Collection, 26, Everett Collection, 27; North Wind Picture
Archives, 12, 25; One Mile Up, Inc., flag, seal 23; Shutterstock: Alex
Pix, cover, alisafarov, bottom right 21, Carol Mellema, 14, Daniel
Prudek, bottom left 21, Deatonphotos, 15, dimair, middle left 21, ekina,
top right 20, Francesco Dazzi, 9, 29, fstockfoto, top right 21, Gerald A.
DeBoer, bottom left 20, Helga Esteb, bottom 19, Jay Petersen, bottom
right 8, John Wollwerth, bottom left 8, Joseph Sohm, 17, joyfuldesigns,
top left 21, Kondor83, bottom right 20, Nagel Photography, 13, photo.
ua, 11, Robert Bohrer, bottom 24, Rosalie Kreulen, middle right 21,
RRuntsch, 7, s_bukley, middle 18, Steven Frame, 5, Tom Grundy, top
24, Zack Frank, 6; Wikimedia: USDA Forest Service, top left 20

All design elements by Shutterstock

Printed and bound in China.
0316/CA21600187
012016 009436F16

TABLE OF CONTENTS

LOCATION...4

GEOGRAPHY...6

WEATHER...8

LANDMARKS..9

HISTORY AND GOVERNMENT..12

INDUSTRY..14

POPULATION...16

FAMOUS PEOPLE...18

STATE SYMBOLS...20

FAST FACTS..22

SOUTH DAKOTA TIMELINE...25

Glossary...30

Read More..31

Internet Sites..31

Critical Thinking Using the Common Core....32

Index..32

Want to take your research further? Ask your librarian if your school subscribes to PebbleGo Next. If so, when you see this helpful symbol 🖱 throughout the book, log onto www.pebblegonext.com for bonus downloads and information.

LOCATION

South Dakota is a midwestern state. North Dakota forms its northern border. Montana and Wyoming lie to the west, and Nebraska is to the south. Iowa and Minnesota form the state's eastern border. South Dakota's capital, Pierre, is in the middle of the state. It's located on the Missouri River. Pierre has fewer than 14,000 people. The largest cities are Sioux Falls, Rapid City, and Aberdeen.

PebbleGo Next Bonus!
To print and label
your own map, go to
www.pebblegonext.com
and search keywords:

SD MAP

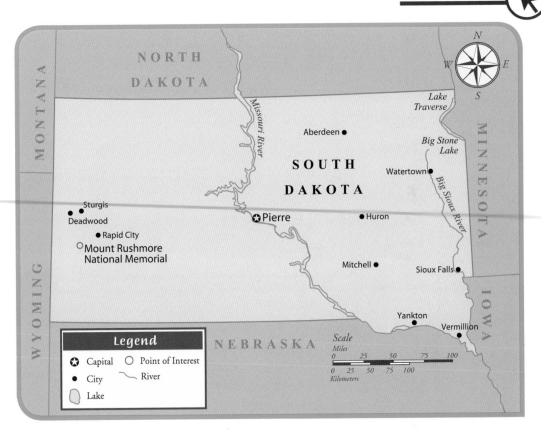

Sioux Falls was named after the waterfalls of the Big Sioux River.

GEOGRAPHY

The Missouri River cuts through South Dakota and divides it nearly in half. Eastern South Dakota has rolling hills and farmland. The Great Plains covers most of western South Dakota.

The Black Hills is a range of low and rugged mountains with deep canyons in the far west. The state's highest point, Harney Peak, is in this region. It is 7,242 feet (2,207 meters) tall.

PebbleGo Next Bonus!
To watch a video about
Mount Rushmore, go to
www.pebblegonext.com
and search keywords:

SD VIDEO

The small, steep hills of the Badlands have very little vegetation.

Harney Peak is the highest peak in the United States east of the Rocky Mountains.

Geographical Center of the United States

GREAT PLAINS

Belle Fourche River

BLACK HILLS

▲ Harney Peak

Missouri River

Cheyenne River

Lake Oahe

Lake Sharpe

BADLANDS NATIONAL PARK

WIND CAVE NATIONAL PARK

Lake Francis Case

Lake Traverse

CENTRAL LOWLANDS

Big Stone Lake

James River

Big Sioux River

Vermillion River

Lewis and Clark Lake

Missouri River

Legend

▲ Highest Point

 Lake

 Mountain Range

 National Park

○ Point of Interest

 River

Scale

Miles
0   25   50   75   100

0   25   50   75   100
Kilometers

WEATHER

Cold winter temperatures differ across the state. In January the northeast averages 10 degrees Fahrenheit (minus 12 degrees Celsius). The southwest averages 22°F (-6°C). Summers can be hot and humid. The western area of the state is drier than the eastern part.

Average High and Low Temperatures (Sioux Falls, SD)

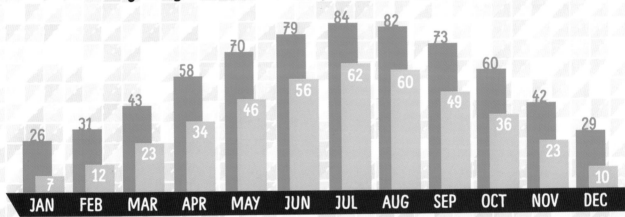

JAN	FEB	MAR	APR	MAY	JUN	JUL	AUG	SEP	OCT	NOV	DEC
26	31	43	58	70	79	84	82	73	60	42	29
7	12	23	34	46	56	62	60	49	36	23	10

Mount Rushmore

It took Gutzon Borglum and his son, Lincoln, more than 14 years to complete the sculptures on Mount Rushmore in South Dakota's Black Hills. Washington's head was completed first. Next came Jefferson, Lincoln, and then Roosevelt.

Crazy Horse Memorial

The world's largest sculpture honors Lakota warrior
Crazy Horse. When the sculpture is finished, it will measure
563 feet (172 m) tall and 641 feet (195 m) long.

Badlands National Park

About 1 million visitors from all around the world visit this national park every year. The park contains fossils that are 35 million years old.

HISTORY AND GOVERNMENT

The Sioux Indians followed the buffalo herds. They were hunters and warriors.

American Indian groups lived in present-day South Dakota before European explorers arrived. The Arikara lived on the northern Great Plains. The Lakota, Nakota, and Dakota Indians lived to the east of the Arikara. They gradually moved west and later became known as the Sioux. French and Spanish fur trappers began moving to the area in the late 1700s.

The Homestead Act of 1862 brought settlers to South Dakota with the promise of free land. The discovery of gold in the Black Hills brought more settlers to the state. In 1889 South Dakota became the 40th state.

South Dakota's government has three branches. The governor leads the executive branch. The legislative branch is made up of the House of Representatives and the Senate. The state has 35 districts, each with one senator and two representatives. The court system in South Dakota is called the Unified Judicial System. It upholds the laws.

In order to save money, the design of South Dakota's capitol building was based on the design of Montana's capitol.

INDUSTRY

Farming is an important industry in South Dakota. Corn is the state's largest crop. Wheat and soybeans are other major crops. South Dakota is the country's second-largest producer of sunflower seeds. Pastures cover about half the state. South Dakota ranchers raise cattle, hogs, and sheep.

Several South Dakota companies process food products. Sioux Falls, Mitchell, and Rapid City have meatpacking plants. Poultry products are processed in Watertown. Dairy products are processed in Aberdeen.

Two types of sunflowers are grown in South Dakota—oilseed and confectionary. Confectionary is used for birdseed and human consumption.

The state's tourism industry is mostly centered in the Black Hills. People from all around the country go there to see the beautiful scenery. People visit natural caves and hike many trails in the mountains. They also camp, hunt, and fish.

Historic Deadwood is a popular tourist destination.

POPULATION

European Americans in South Dakota are mostly descended from Norwegian, German, Irish, Czech, and English settlers. Most of these European immigrants arrived in the 1800s. The nine Indian tribes in South Dakota are all part of the Great Sioux Nation. Indian reservations cover much of the state. American Indians make up almost 10 percent of the state's population.

Population by Ethnicity

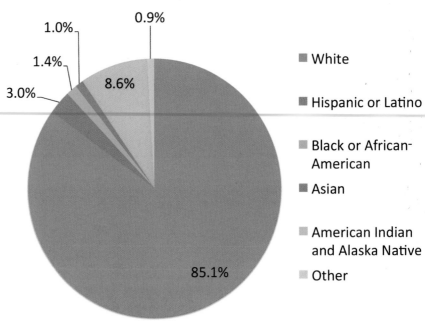

1.0%
1.4%
3.0%
8.6%
0.9%
85.1%

- White
- Hispanic or Latino
- Black or African-American
- Asian
- American Indian and Alaska Native
- Other

Source: U.S. Census Bureau.

FAMOUS PEOPLE

Mike Miller (1980–) played for the NBA's Miami Heat when they won the championship in 2012 and 2013. He grew up in Mitchell.

Tom Brokaw (1940–) is a former TV news reporter. He hosted the NBC Nightly News until he retired in 2004. He was born in Webster.

Laura Ingalls Wilder (1867–1957) wrote many children's books. *The Long Winter, Little Town on the Prairie*, and *By the Shores of Silver Lake* tell about her time in De Smet.

Crazy Horse (circa 1849–1877) was an Oglala Sioux chief. He defended the Black Hills and fought in Montana's Battle of the Little Bighorn. He defeated General George Crook at the Battle of Rosebud Creek.

Sitting Bull (1831–1890) was a Hunkpapa Lakota chief and spiritual leader. Sitting Bull led his people against General Custer at the Battle of the Little Bighorn in Montana.

January Jones (1978–) is an actress and model. She has appeared in many movies and has received Emmy and Golden Globe nominations for her role in the TV show *Mad Men*. She was born in Sioux Falls.

STATE SYMBOLS

Tree

Black Hills spruce

Flower

American pasqueflower

Bird

Chinese ring-necked pheasant

Fish

walleye

PebbleGo Next Bonus! To make a treat using one of South Dakota's leading crops, go to www.pebblegonext.com and search keywords:

SD RECIPE

Jewelry

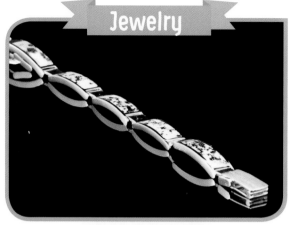

Black Hills gold

Sport

rodeo

Fossil

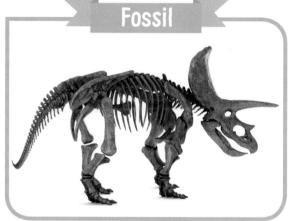

triceratops

Animal

coyote

Insect

honeybee

Dessert

kuchen

FAST FACTS

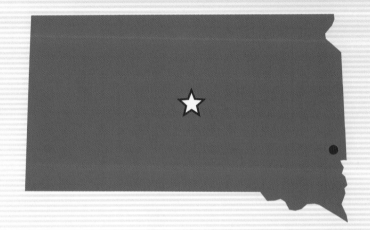

STATEHOOD
1889

CAPITAL ☆
Pierre

LARGEST CITY •
Sioux Falls

SIZE
75,811 square miles (196,350 square kilometers) land area
(2010 U.S. Census Bureau)

POPULATION
844,877 (2013 U.S. Census estimate)

STATE NICKNAME
Mount Rushmore State

STATE MOTTO
"Under God, the people rule"

STATE SEAL

The state seal represents life in South Dakota. An image of the Missouri River flows through the middle of the seal. The dark mountains in the background stand for the Black Hills. A farmer plowing a field shows that farming is important in South Dakota. Cattle represent the ranching industry. A mill and furnace on the left side of the river stand for manufacturing. The date 1889 is the year South Dakota became a state.

PebbleGo Next Bonus!
To print and color your own flag, go to www.pebblegonext.com and search keywords:

SD FLAG

STATE FLAG

The South Dakota state flag is blue and features the state seal surrounded by a golden sun. The state seal represents life in South Dakota and includes the Missouri River, the Black Hills, farming, ranching, and manufacturing. The state name and its official nickname circle the seal. The current flag was adopted in 1992. That year, the nickname changed from the Sunshine State to the Mount Rushmore State.

MINING PRODUCTS

gold, lime, limestone

MANUFACTURED GOODS

machinery, food products, chemicals, metal, motor vehicle parts, computer and electronic equipment

FARM PRODUCTS

corn, soybeans, wheat, sunflower seeds, cattle, hogs, sheep

To learn the lyrics to the state song, go to www.pebblegonext.com and search keywords:

SD SONG

SOUTH DAKOTA TIMELINE

1600s Sioux Indians are living in what is now South Dakota.

1620 The Pilgrims establish a colony in the New World in present-day Massachusetts.

1743 Louis-Joseph and Francois La Verendrye become the first European explorers to see South Dakota.

1804 Meriwether Lewis and William Clark explore the Missouri River in South Dakota.

1861 Dakota Territory is established.

1861–1865 The Union and the Confederacy fight the Civil War.

1877 The Sioux Treaty gives the Black Hills to the United States.

1889 South Dakota becomes the 40th state on November 2.

1890 U.S. soldiers kill hundreds of Sioux at Wounded Knee.

1914–1918 World War I is fought; the United States enters the war in 1917.

1927 Work begins on Mount Rushmore National Memorial in the Black Hills.

1939–1945 World War II is fought; the United States enters the war in 1941.

1973 Members of the American Indian Movement and other Indians take over the Wounded Knee village.

1980 The U.S. Supreme Court rules that the U.S. government must pay the Sioux $106 million for the Black Hills; the Sioux refuse the money.

1996 Governor Bill Janklow starts a program to bring technology and Internet access to all schools in the state.

1998 The face of Crazy Horse on the Crazy Horse Memorial is completed.

2007 Homestake, a former gold mine near Lead, becomes a deep underground science and engineering laboratory.

2011 Mount Rushmore National Memorial marks the 70th anniversary of its completion.

2015 South Dakota has the driest January to April ever recorded, receiving only 42 percent of its average precipitation for spring.

Glossary

defend *(di-FEND)*—to try to keep someone or something from being changed or harmed

descend *(dee-SEND)*—to belong to a later generation of the same family

executive *(ig-ZE-kyuh-tiv)*—the branch of government that makes sure laws are followed

fossil *(FOSS-uhl)*—the remains or traces of an animal or a plant from millions of years ago, preserved as rock

immigrant *(IM-uh-gruhnt)*—someone who comes from abroad to live permanently in a country

industry *(IN-duh-stree)*—a business which produces a product or provides a service

judicial *(joo-DISH-uhl)*—to do with the branch of government that explains and interprets the laws

legislature *(LEJ-iss-lay-chur)*—a group of elected officials who have the power to make or change laws for a country or state

rancher *(RANCH-ur)*—a person who owns or works on a ranch

reservation *(rez-er-VAY-shuhn)*—an area of land set aside by the U.S. government for American Indians

tourism *(TOOR-i-zuhm)*—the business of taking care of visitors to a country or place

Read More

Bjorklund, Ruth. *South Dakota*. It's My State! New York: Cavendish Square Publishing, 2016.

Ganeri, Anita. *United States of America: A Benjamin Blog and His Inquisitive Dog Guide*. Country Guides. Chicago: Heinemann Raintree, 2015.

Meinking, Mary. *What's Great About South Dakota?* Our Great States. Minneapolis: Lerner Publications Company, 2015.

Internet Sites

FactHound offers a safe, fun way to find Internet sites related to this book. All of the sites on FactHound have been researched by our staff.

Here's all you do:

Visit *www.facthound.com*

Type in this code: 9781515704294

 Check out projects, games and lots more at **www.capstonekids.com**

Critical Thinking Using the Common Core

1. What four presidents are carved into Mount Rushmore? (Key Ideas and Details)

2. Which American Indian tribes became known as the Sioux? (Key Ideas and Details)

3. The Badlands National Park contains fossils that are 35 million years old. What is a fossil? (Craft and Structure)

Index

American Indians, 12, 16, 19, 26, 27, 28

capital, 4, 22

ethnicities, 16

famous people, 18–19
farming, 14, 24

government, 13, 28
Great Plains, 6, 12

history, 12, 23, 25–29
Homestead Act, 12

industries, 14–15, 24

landmarks, 9–11
  Badlands National Park, 11
  Crazy Horse Memorial, 10, 28
  Mount Rushmore, 9, 27, 29

Missouri River, 4, 6, 23, 25
mountains, 6, 15, 23
  Black Hills, 6, 9, 12, 15, 19, 23, 26, 27, 28

population, 16, 22

state symbols, 20–21, 23

weather, 8, 29